THE LEFT-HANDER'S

2012 CALENDAR

BY CARY KOEGLE

Left-handed legends, lore & more

Andrews McMeel
Publishing, LLC
City • Sydney • London

December 2011								January 2012					
S	M	T	W	T	F	S	S	M	T	W	T	F	S
				1	2	3	1	2	3	4	5	6	7
4	5	6	7	8	9	10	8	9	10	11	12	13	14
11	12	13	14	15	16	17	15	16	17	18	19	20	21
18	19	20	21	22	23	24	22	23	24	25	26	27	28
25	26	27	28	29	30	31	29	30	31				

"The left stuff" is all of that out-of-the-box stuff. The trait grants those who possess it a tendency toward more flexible thinking, the psychological freedom to question orthodoxies, and the cognitive facility to update beliefs.

—Melissa Roth, *The Left Stuff*

DEC 2011-JAN 2012

Monday

26

Kwanzaa begins (USA)
Christmas Day (observed) (UK, Australia—except TAS, VIC)
Boxing Day (Canada, NZ, Australia—TAS, VIC)
St. Stephen's Day (Ireland)

Tuesday

27

Christmas Day (observed) (Ireland, NZ, Australia—TAS, VIC)
Boxing Day (observed) (UK, Australia—except SA, TAS, VIC)
Proclamation Day (Australia—SA)

Wednesday

28

Hanukkah ends

Thursday

29

Friday

30

Saturday

31

Sunday

1

New Year's Day
Kwanzaa ends (USA)
Lefty birthday: **guitarist Eric Gales**

January 2012

S	M	T	W	T	F	S
1	2	3	4	5	6	7
8	9	10	11	12	13	14
15	16	17	18	19	20	21
22	23	24	25	26	27	28
29	30	31				

Lefty Lore

A Danish legend says that on the twelfth night after Christmas, if an unmarried woman walks to bed backward, throws a shoe over her left shoulder, and says a verse to the Three Holy Kings, the man she sees in her dreams will one day marry her.

JANUARY

Monday

2

New Year's Day (observed)
(Ireland, NZ, UK, Australia)

Tuesday

3

Bank Holiday (UK—Scotland)

Wednesday

4

Lefty birthday: **singer Michael Stipe**

Thursday

5

Lefty birthday: **actress Diane Keaton**

Friday

6

Saturday

7

Sunday

8

Lefty birthday: **singer David Bowie**

January 2012

S	M	T	W	T	F	S
1	2	3	4	5	6	7
8	9	10	11	12	13	14
15	16	17	18	19	20	21
22	23	24	25	26	27	28
29	30	31				

Left-handed tennis player Monica Seles was born in Novi Sad, Yugoslavia. She started playing tennis at age five, became an American citizen in 1994, and won a bronze medal at the 2000 Summer Olympics. Her powerful shots and trademark grunt have also earned her nine Grand Slam titles. Seles uses both her left and right when hitting forehands and backhands, but her main thrust comes from the left. She announced her retirement in 2008 and was inducted into the International Tennis Hall of Fame in 2009.

JANUARY

Monday

9

Lefty birthday: artist Ronnie Landfield

Tuesday

10

Lefty birthday: baseball player Willie McCovey

Wednesday

11

Lefty birthday: first secretary of the treasury Alexander Hamilton

Thursday

12

Friday

13

Saturday

14

Lefty birthday: doctor and missionary Albert Schweitzer

Sunday

15

Lefty birthday: civil rights activist Martin Luther King Jr.

January 2012

S	M	T	W	T	F	S
1	2	3	4	5	6	7
8	9	10	11	12	13	14
15	16	17	18	19	20	21
22	23	24	25	26	27	28
29	30	31				

Inspiration from Lefties

Darkness cannot drive out darkness; only light can do that. Hate cannot drive out hate; only love can do that.

—Martin Luther King Jr.

JANUARY

Monday

16

Martin Luther King Jr.'s Birthday (observed) (USA)

Tuesday

17

Lefty birthday: **inventor and statesman Benjamin Franklin**

Wednesday

18

Lefty birthday: **actor Cary Grant**

Thursday

19

Lefty birthday: **singer Phil Everly**

Friday

20

Lefty birthday: **astronaut Buzz Aldrin**

Saturday

21

Sunday

22

Lefty birthday: **actress Diane Lane**

January 2012

S	M	T	W	T	F	S
	1	2	3	4	5	6	7
8	9	10	11	12	13	14
15	16	17	18	19	20	21
22	23	24	25	26	27	28
29	30	31				

Lefty Artists

Albrecht Dürer

Hans Holbein

Paul Klee

LeRoy Neiman

Raphael

JANUARY

Monday

23

Lefty birthday: **tennis player Petr Korda**

Tuesday

24

Wednesday

25

Lefty birthday: **actress Christine Lakin**

Thursday

26

Australia Day

Friday

27

Lefty birthday: **author Lewis Carroll**

Saturday

28

Lefty birthday: **physicist August Piccard**

Sunday

29

Lefty birthday: **media mogul Oprah Winfrey**

January 2012								February 2012					
S	M	T	W	T	F	S		S	M	T	W	T	F	S
1	2	3	4	5	6	7					1	2	3	4
8	9	10	11	12	13	14		5	6	7	8	9	10	11
15	16	17	18	19	20	21		12	13	14	15	16	17	18
22	23	24	25	26	27	28		19	20	21	22	23	24	25
29	30	31						26	27	28	29			

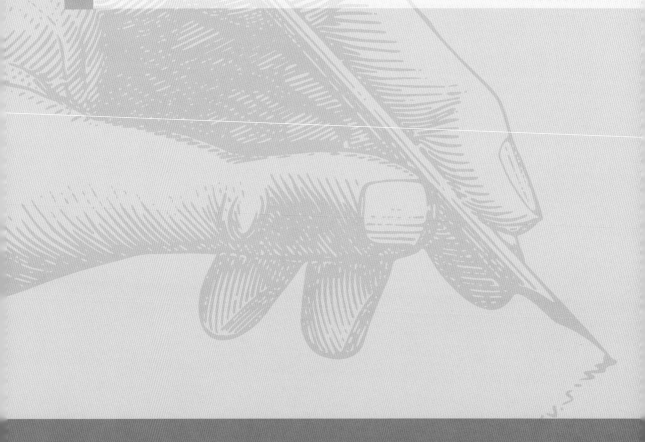

Are You Really Left-Handed?

Drop a pen on the ground. The hand you pick the pen up with is usually your dominant hand.

JANUARY-FEBRUARY

Monday

30

Lefty birthday: singer Phil Collins

Tuesday

31

Lefty birthday: bowler Patty Costello

Wednesday

1

Lefty birthday: singer Don Everly

Thursday

2

Friday

3

Saturday

4

Lefty birthday: boxer Oscar de la Hoya

Sunday

5

Lefty birthday: novelist and actress Mandy Rice-Davies

February 2012

S	M	T	W	T	F	S
			1	2	3	4
5	6	7	8	9	10	11
12	13	14	15	16	17	18
19	20	21	22	23	24	25
26	27	28	29			

Musical scholar, organist, doctor, missionary, and philosopher, Albert Schweitzer taught himself to write effectively with his right hand, so he would not disturb his cat, Sizi, who made a habit of falling asleep on Schweitzer's left hand whenever he was at his desk working. This multi-talented lefty received the Nobel Peace Prize in 1952. His lecture, "The Problem of Peace," is still considered one of the best speeches ever given.

FEBRUARY

Monday
6

Waitangi Day (NZ)

Tuesday
7

Wednesday
8

Lefty birthday: journalist Ted Koppel

Thursday
9

Lefty birthday: baseball player John Kruk

Friday
10

Lefty birthday: Olympic swimmer Mark Spitz

Saturday
11

Lefty birthday: inventor Thomas Edison

Sunday
12

Lefty birthday: basketball player Bill Russell

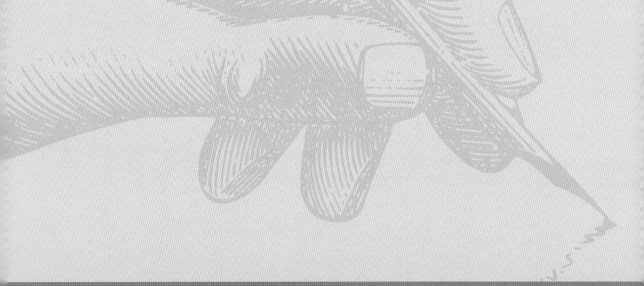

February 2012

S	M	T	W	T	F	S
			1	2	3	4
5	6	7	8	9	10	11
12	13	14	15	16	17	18
19	20	21	22	23	24	25
26	27	28	29			

The Quotable Lefty

"While right-handed people rarely think about which hand another person is using, lefties are quick to spot a fellow southpaw. We've been watching other members of our exclusive club since the beginning of recorded history."

—Rae Lindsay, *Left Is Right*

FEBRUARY

Monday
13

Lefty birthday: **actress Kim Novak**

Tuesday
14

St. Valentine's Day

Wednesday
15

Lefty birthday: **cartoonist Matt Groening**

Thursday
16

Lefty birthday: **tennis player John McEnroe**

Friday
17

Saturday
18

Lefty birthday: **actor Matt Dillon**

Sunday
19

Lefty birthday: **singer Seal**

February 2012

S	M	T	W	T	F	S
			1	2	3	4
5	6	7	8	9	10	11
12	13	14	15	16	17	18
19	20	21	22	23	24	25
26	27	28	29			

Highlights from the History of Left-Handedness

1508: At only thirty-three, left-handed artist Michelangelo started painting the ceiling of the Sistine Chapel for Pope Julius II.

FEBRUARY

Monday
20

Presidents' Day (USA)
Lefty birthday: **singer Kurt Cobain**

Tuesday
21

Lefty birthday: **baseball player John Titus**

Wednesday
22

Ash Wednesday

Thursday
23

Lefty birthday: **actor Peter Fonda**

Friday
24

Saturday
25

Lefty birthday: **opera singer Enrico Caruso**

Sunday
26

| February 2012 |
S	M	T	W	T	F	S
			1	2	3	4
5	6	7	8	9	10	11
12	13	14	15	16	17	18
19	20	21	22	23	24	25
26	27	28	29			

| March 2012 |
S	M	T	W	T	F	S
				1	2	3
4	5	6	7	8	9	10
11	12	13	14	15	16	17
18	19	20	21	22	23	24
25	26	27	28	29	30	31

Lefty Fun Fact

Did you know that there is a Facebook page for lefties? It's the "Left-Handed People Society," and is a group "for all of those left-handed people out there and also those who just really admire people who are left-handed!"

FEBRUARY-MARCH

Monday

27

Lefty birthday: **actress Joanne Woodward**

Tuesday

28

Lefty birthday: **scientist Linus Pauling**

Wednesday

29

Thursday

1

St. David's Day (UK)

Friday

2

Lefty birthday: **baseball player Mel Ott**

Saturday

3

Lefty birthday: **cartoonist Ronald Searle**

Sunday

4

March 2012

S	M	T	W	T	F	S
				1	2	3
4	5	6	7	8	9	10
11	12	13	14	15	16	17
18	19	20	21	22	23	24
25	26	27	28	29	30	31

*Begins at sundown the previous day

Inspiration from Lefties

Ask yourself: Have you been kind today? Make kindness your daily modus operandi and change your world.

—Annie Lennox

MARCH

Monday

5

Labour Day (Australia—WA)

Tuesday

6

Lefty birthday: **artist Michelangelo**

Wednesday

7

Lefty birthday: **composer Maurice Ravel**

Thursday

8

Purim*
International Women's Day

Friday

9

Saturday

10

Lefty birthday: **Left-Hander's International
founder Dean R. Campbell**

Sunday

11

Lefty birthday: **actor Peter Berg**

March 2012

S	M	T	W	T	F	S
				1	2	3
4	5	6	7	8	9	10
11	12	13	14	15	16	17
18	19	20	21	22	23	24
25	26	27	28	29	30	31

The Left Stuff

Being Left-Handed, a Web site by E. Stephen Mack, offers information, discussion, and resources for lefties, including a simple explanation for elementary school students on what it's like to be a lefty. All this and more can be found at www.42inc.com/~estephen/facts/lefthand.html.

MARCH

Monday
12

Eight Hours Day (Australia—TAS)
Labour Day (Australia—VIC)
Canberra Day (Australia—ACT)
Commonwealth Day (Australia, Canada, NZ, UK)

Tuesday
13

Wednesday
14

Lefty birthday: **physicist Albert Einstein**

Thursday
15

Lefty birthday: **Supreme Court justice
Ruth Bader Ginsburg**

Friday
16

Lefty birthday: **actor Victor Garber**

Saturday
17

St. Patrick's Day

Sunday
18

Mothering Sunday (Ireland, UK)

March 2012

S	M	T	W	T	F	S
				1	2	3
4	5	6	7	8	9	10
11	12	13	14	15	16	17
18	19	20	21	22	23	24
25	26	27	28	29	30	31

Born on March 23, left-handed Egyptian pharaoh Ramesses II built more monuments, temples, and major statues than any other Egyptian king. Known by his successors as the "Great Ancestor," he died at around ninety years of age, outliving many of his wives and children. His sixty-seven-year reign marks the last peak of Egypt's imperial power.

MARCH

Monday

19

Lefty birthday: actor Bruce Willis

Tuesday

20

Lefty birthday: director Spike Lee

Wednesday

21

Lefty birthday: actor Matthew Broderick

Thursday

22

Friday

23

Saturday

24

Lefty birthday: fashion designer Tommy Hilfiger

Sunday

25

Lefty birthday: actress Sarah Jessica Parker

March 2012						
S	M	T	W	T	F	S
				1	2	3
4	5	6	7	8	9	10
11	12	13	14	15	16	17
18	19	20	21	22	23	24
25	26	27	28	29	30	31

April 2012						
S	M	T	W	T	F	S
1	2	3	4	5	6	7
8	9	10	11	12	13	14
15	16	17	18	19	20	21
22	23	24	25	26	27	28
29	30					

Rock and Roll Lefties

David Bowie

Billy Corgan

Jimi Hendrix

Joan Jett

Robert Plant

MARCH-APRIL

Monday
26

Lefty birthday: **actor James Caan**

Tuesday
27

Lefty birthday: **Prince Louis XVIII**

Wednesday
28

Lefty birthday: **actress Dianne Wiest**

Thursday
29

Lefty birthday: **baseball player Eric Gunderson**

Friday
30

Lefty birthday: **singer Celine Dion**

Saturday
31

Lefty birthday: **congressman Barney Frank**

Sunday
1

Palm Sunday

April 2012

S	M	T	W	T	F	S
1	2	3	4	5	6	7
8	9	10	11	12	13	14
15	16	17	18	19	20	21
22	23	24	25	26	27	28
29	30					

*Begins at sundown the previous day

Name the Lefties

Q: What two lefty musicians worked together on the
   "Feed the World" project and the Live Aid Concert?
   One was the organizer of both events, the other was
   a performer.

A: Bob Geldolf and Sting

APRIL

Monday

2

Lefty birthday: author Hans Christian Anderson

Tuesday

3

Lefty birthday: actress Marsha Mason

Wednesday

4

Lefty birthday: actress Cloris Leachman

Thursday

5

Lefty birthday: former secretary of state Colin Powell

Friday

6

Good Friday (Western)

Saturday

7

Passover*
Easter Saturday (Australia—except TAS, WA)

Sunday

8

Easter (Western)

April 2012

S	M	T	W	T	F	S
1	2	3	4	5	6	7
8	9	10	11	12	13	14
15	16	17	18	19	20	21
22	23	24	25	26	27	28
29	30					

Highlights from the History of Left-Handedness

1964: The Beatles arrived in the United States for the first time. Half of the members of the Fab Four are lefties—Paul McCartney and Ringo Starr.

APRIL

Monday
9

Easter Monday (Australia, Canada, Ireland, NZ, UK—except Scotland)

Tuesday
10

Lefty birthday: **actor Chuck Connors**

Wednesday
11

Lefty birthday: **actress Louise Lasser**

Thursday
12

Lefty birthday: **singer Tiny Tim**

Friday
13

Holy Friday (Orthodox)

Saturday
14

Passover ends

Sunday
15

Easter (Orthodox)

April 2012						
S	M	T	W	T	F	S
1	2	3	4	5	6	7
8	9	10	11	12	13	14
15	16	17	18	19	20	21
22	23	24	25	26	27	28
29	30					

Born in Georgia, Michael Stipe grew up as an army brat. The lead vocalist for the alternative rock band R.E.M. is also a political activist and photographer. Some of Stipe's charity support has helped raise funds for Amnesty International, PETA, and Hurricane Katrina victims. This talented lefty also runs his own film production companies, producing such films as *Velvet Goldmine*, *Thirteen Conversations about One Thing*, and the Oscar-nominated *Being John Malkovich*.

APRIL

Monday

16

Lefty birthday: actor Charlie Chaplin

Tuesday

17

Lefty birthday: football player Norman "Boomer" Esiason

Wednesday

18

Lefty birthday: lawyer Clarence Darrow

Thursday

19

Lefty birthday: actress Kate Hudson

Friday

20

Lefty birthday: baseball player Don Mattingly

Saturday

21

Sunday

22

Earth Day

April 2012

S	M	T	W	T	F	S
1	2	3	4	5	6	7
8	9	10	11	12	13	14
15	16	17	18	19	20	21
22	23	24	25	26	27	28
29	30					

Lefty Language

Aristera, or "left" in Greek, means "the best." It is also the root of the English word "aristocratic." And in Japanese, the word for left is *hidari*. It also means "sun" and "on."

APRIL

Monday

23

St. George's Day (UK)

Tuesday

24

Lefty birthday: **actress Shirley MacLaine**

Wednesday

25

Anzac Day (NZ, Australia)

Thursday

26

Lefty birthday: **comedienne Carol Burnett**

Friday

27

Lefty birthday: **bowler Earl Anthony**

Saturday

28

Lefty birthday: **talk show host Jay Leno**

Sunday

29

Lefty birthday: **comedian Jerry Seinfeld**

April 2012						
S	M	T	W	T	F	S
1	2	3	4	5	6	7
8	9	10	11	12	13	14
15	16	17	18	19	20	21
22	23	24	25	26	27	28
29	30					

May 2012						
S	M	T	W	T	F	S
		1	2	3	4	5
6	7	8	9	10	11	12
13	14	15	16	17	18	19
20	21	22	23	24	25	26
27	28	29	30	31		

The Quotable Lefty

"No one hit home runs the way Babe [Ruth] did. They were something special. They were like homing pigeons. The ball would leave the bat, pause briefly, suddenly gain its bearings, then take off for the stands."

—Lefty Gomez

APRIL-MAY

Monday

30

Tuesday

1

Lefty birthday: Arthur William Patrick Albert, Duke of Connaught and Strathearn

Wednesday

2

Lefty birthday: Olympic figure skater Sarah Hughes

Thursday

3

Lefty birthday: singer James Brown

Friday

4

Lefty birthday: baseball player Virne Beatrice "Jackie" Mitchell

Saturday

5

Sunday

6

Lefty birthday: actress Mare Winningham

May 2012

S	M	T	W	T	F	S
		1	2	3	4	5
6	7	8	9	10	11	12
13	14	15	16	17	18	19
20	21	22	23	24	25	26
27	28	29	30	31		

You've Come a Long Way, Lefty

- Today, if you choose to write with your left hand, in most schools you'll be encouraged, not switched.
- Once scarce, left-handed scissors are now common in kindergarten.
- No one raises an eyebrow when you request the outside left-handed place setting in a restaurant or at a dinner party.

MAY

Monday
7

Labour Day (Australia—QLD)
May Day (Australia—NT)
Early May Bank Holiday (Ireland, UK)

Tuesday
8

Lefty birthday: **former president Harry S. Truman**

Wednesday
9

Thursday
10

Lefty birthday: **dancer Fred Astaire**

Friday
11

Lefty birthday: **football player Matt Leinart**

Saturday
12

Lefty birthday: **baseball player Yogi Berra**

Sunday
13

Mother's Day (USA, Australia, Canada, NZ)

May 2012

S	M	T	W	T	F	S
		1	2	3	4	5
6	7	8	9	10	11	12
13	14	15	16	17	18	19
20	21	22	23	24	25	26
27	28	29	30	31		

Inspiration from Lefties

Logic will get you from A to B. Imagination will take you everywhere.

—Albert Einstein

MAY

Monday

14

Lefty birthday: singer David Byrne

Tuesday

15

Lefty birthday: baseball player George Brett

Wednesday

16

Thursday

17

Lefty birthday: Arthur Wellesley,
General and Duke of Wellington

Friday

18

Lefty birthday: actress Tina Fey

Saturday

19

Armed Forces Day (USA)

Sunday

20

Lefty birthday: comedian George Gobel

May 2012

S	M	T	W	T	F	S
		1	2	3	4	5
6	7	8	9	10	11	12
13	14	15	16	17	18	19
20	21	22	23	24	25	26
27	28	29	30	31		

Peggy Guggenheim was known as the "Mistress of Modern Art." While living in Paris in the 1920s, she became friendly with many avant-garde writers and artists and by the late 1930s was beginning to collect works. She established her collection in Venice, Italy, loaned it out to museums throughout Europe and America, and eventually donated her large home and her collection to the Solomon R. Guggenheim Foundation upon her death in 1979.

MAY

Monday

21

Victoria Day (Canada)

Tuesday

22

Lefty birthday: conductor Peter Nero

Wednesday

23

Lefty birthday: *Jeopardy!* winner Ken Jennings

Thursday

24

Lefty birthday: singer Bob Dylan

Friday

25

Saturday

26

Lefty birthday: singer Lauryn Hill

Sunday

27

Lefty birthday: lawman Wild Bill Hickok

May 2012						
S	M	T	W	T	F	S
		1	2	3	4	5
6	7	8	9	10	11	12
13	14	15	16	17	18	19
20	21	22	23	24	25	26
27	28	29	30	31		

June 2012						
S	M	T	W	T	F	S
					1	2
3	4	5	6	7	8	9
10	11	12	13	14	15	16
17	18	19	20	21	22	23
24	25	26	27	28	29	30

Lefties Playing Lefties

Rocky Balboa, played by Sylvester Stallone in *Rocky*

Julius Caesar, played by Rex Harrison in *Cleopatra*

George Costanza, played by Jason Alexander on *Seinfeld*

MAY-JUNE

Monday

28

Memorial Day (USA)
Spring Bank Holiday (UK—Scotland)

Tuesday

29

Wednesday

30

Lefty birthday: **football player Gale Sayers**

Thursday

31

Lefty birthday: **actor Jim Hutton**

Friday

1

Lefty birthday: **actress Marilyn Monroe**

Saturday

2

Sunday

3

Lefty birthday: **tennis player Rafael Nadal**

June 2012

S	M	T	W	T	F	S
					1	2
3	4	5	6	7	8	9
10	11	12	13	14	15	16
17	18	19	20	21	22	23
24	25	26	27	28	29	30

The proportion of left-handers in Britain has increased more than fourfold over the past one hundred years and may rise further, possibly bringing a surge of musical, mathematical, and sporting prodigies.

—Jonathan Leake and Jack Grimston,
The Sunday Times, March 17, 2002

JUNE

Monday

4

Tuesday

5

Wednesday

6

Thursday

7

Lefty birthday: **musician Prince**

Friday

8

Lefty birthday: **artist LeRoy Neiman**

Saturday

9

Lefty birthday: **composer Cole Porter**

Sunday

10

June 2012

S	M	T	W	T	F	S
					1	2
3	4	5	6	7	8	9
10	11	12	13	14	15	16
17	18	19	20	21	22	23
24	25	26	27	28	29	30

Sporty Father and Son Lefties

Fencers Giuseppe and Edoardo Mangiarotti

Golfers Russ and Ryan Cochran

Hockey players Bobby and Brett Hull

JUNE

Monday

11

Queen's Birthday (Australia—except WA)

Tuesday

12

Lefty birthday: **former president George H.W. Bush**

Wednesday

13

Lefty birthday: **actor Tim Allen**

Thursday

14

Flag Day (USA)

Friday

15

Lefty birthday: **jazz musician Errol Garner**

Saturday

16

Sunday

17

Father's Day (USA, Canada, Ireland, UK)

June 2012

S	M	T	W	T	F	S
					1	2
3	4	5	6	7	8	9
10	11	12	13	14	15	16
17	18	19	20	21	22	23
24	25	26	27	28	29	30

As the child of a U.S. diplomat, actor Greg Kinnear moved around often. In fact, he began his career in Greece. While a student in Athens, he had his own radio show, "School Daze with Greg Kinnear." He received an Emmy in 1995 for *Talk Soup* and in 1998 was nominated for an Oscar for his role in *As Good As It Gets*. Most recently this southpaw starred in *Little Miss Sunshine*, *Invincible*, *Baby Mama*, and *The Last Song*.

JUNE

Monday

18

Lefty birthday: singer/songwriter Paul McCartney

Tuesday

19

Lefty birthday: baseball player Lou Gehrig

Wednesday

20

Lefty birthday: actress Nicole Kidman

Thursday

21

Lefty birthday: Prince William of Wales

Friday

22

Saturday

23

Lefty birthday: Empress Josephine of France

Sunday

24

June 2012						
S	M	T	W	T	F	S
					1	2
3	4	5	6	7	8	9
10	11	12	13	14	15	16
17	18	19	20	21	22	23
24	25	26	27	28	29	30

July 2012						
S	M	T	W	T	F	S
1	2	3	4	5	6	7
8	9	10	11	12	13	14
15	16	17	18	19	20	21
22	23	24	25	26	27	28
29	30	31				

The Left Stuff

No need to use a backward oven mitt for barbecuing. At leftyslefthanded.com, you can buy your favorite lefty a mitt that announces, "I may be left-handed, but I'm always right!" This mitt protects the left hand and arm with a back constructed of heat-resistant, quilted fabric.

JUNE-JULY

Monday

25

Lefty birthday: basketball player Willis Reed

Tuesday

26

Lefty birthday: singer Chris Isaak

Wednesday

27

Lefty birthday: writer and lecturer Helen Keller

Thursday

28

Friday

29

Lefty birthday: producer/director Stanley Ralph Ross

Saturday

30

Lefty birthday: oceanographer Robert D. Ballard

Sunday

1

Canada Day

July 2012

S	M	T	W	T	F	S
1	2	3	4	5	6	7
8	9	10	11	12	13	14
15	16	17	18	19	20	21
22	23	24	25	26	27	28
29	30	31				

Political Lefties

Michael Bloomberg

George H.W. Bush

Winston Churchill

Bill Clinton

Alexander Hamilton

Benjamin Netanyahu

Barack Obama

JULY

Monday

2

Tuesday

3

Lefty birthday: **humorist Dave Barry**

Wednesday

4

Independence Day (USA)

Thursday

5

Lefty birthday: **Davis Cup founder Dwight Davis**

Friday

6

Lefty birthday: **actor Sylvester Stallone**

Saturday

7

Lefty birthday: **musician Ringo Starr**

Sunday

8

Lefty birthday: **former vice president Nelson Rockefeller**

July 2012

S	M	T	W	T	F	S
1	2	3	4	5	6	7
8	9	10	11	12	13	14
15	16	17	18	19	20	21
22	23	24	25	26	27	28
29	30	31				

Lefty Lore

Palmists look at the left or right hand to read different
characteristics. Your left hand is said to reveal your
private side—your fantasies, hopes, and dreams.

JULY

Monday
9

Lefty birthday: **inventor Elias Howe**

Tuesday
10

Lefty birthday: **boxer John Sholto Douglas**

Wednesday
11

Thursday
12

Lefty birthday: **fitness guru Richard Simmons**

Friday
13

Lefty birthday: **chef Paul Prudhomme**

Saturday
14

Lefty birthday: **former president Gerald Ford**

Sunday
15

July 2012

S	M	T	W	T	F	S
1	2	3	4	5	6	7
8	9	10	11	12	13	14
15	16	17	18	19	20	21
22	23	24	25	26	27	28
29	30	31				

Nicknamed "The Kid," "The Splendid Splinter," "Teddy Ballgame," and "The Thumper," baseball great and left-hander Ted Williams played nineteen seasons, twice interrupted by military service as a Marine Corps pilot, with the Boston Red Sox. Williams was inducted into the Baseball Hall of Fame in 1966. Also an avid sport fisherman, he hosted a television show about fishing and was inducted into the Fishing Hall of Fame in 2000.

JULY

Monday
16

Lefty birthday: comedian Will Ferrell

Tuesday
17

Wednesday
18

Lefty birthday: author Jessamyn West

Thursday
19

Friday
20

Ramadan

Saturday
21

Lefty birthday: author Marshall McLuhan

Sunday
22

Lefty birthday: actor David Spade

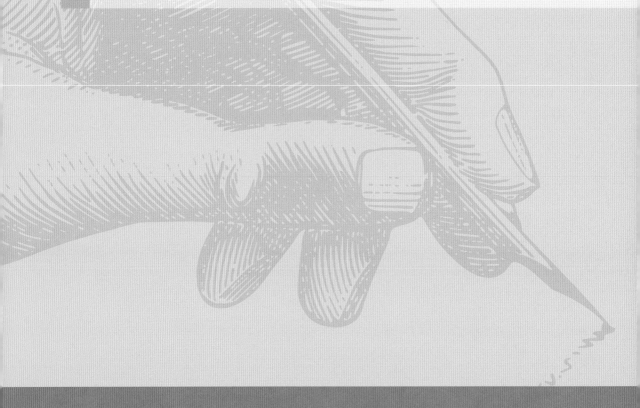

July 2012

S	M	T	W	T	F	S
1	2	3	4	5	6	7
8	9	10	11	12	13	14
15	16	17	18	19	20	21
22	23	24	25	26	27	28
29	30	31				

Inspiration from Lefties

A dream doesn't become reality through magic; it takes sweat, determination, and hard work.

—Secretary of State Colin Powell

JULY

Monday

23

Lefty birthday: actor Omar Epps

Tuesday

24

Lefty birthday: political cartoonist Pat Oliphant

Wednesday

25

Thursday

26

Lefty birthday: Olympic figure skater Dorothy Hamill

Friday

27

Lefty birthday: cricket player Alan Border

Saturday

28

Lefty birthday: basketball player and politician Bill Bradley

Sunday

29

July 2012						
S	M	T	W	T	F	S
1	2	3	4	5	6	7
8	9	10	11	12	13	14
15	16	17	18	19	20	21
22	23	24	25	26	27	28
29	30	31				

August 2012						
S	M	T	W	T	F	S
			1	2	3	4
5	6	7	8	9	10	11
12	13	14	15	16	17	18
19	20	21	22	23	24	25
26	27	28	29	30	31	

Lefty Names Before and After

Nathan Birnbaum (George Burns)

Frances Gumm (Judy Garland)

Caryn Johnson (Whoopi Goldberg)

Gordon Matthew Sumner (Sting)

Robert Zimmerman (Bob Dylan)

JULY-AUGUST

Monday

30

Lefty birthday: actress Lisa Kudrow

Tuesday

31

Lefty birthday: actor Barry Van Dyke

Wednesday

1

Lefty birthday: game show host Allen Ludden

Thursday

2

Lefty birthday: author James Baldwin

Friday

3

Saturday

4

Lefty birthday: President Barack Obama

Sunday

5

August 2012

S	M	T	W	T	F	S
			1	2	3	4
5	6	7	8	9	10	11
12	13	14	15	16	17	18
19	20	21	22	23	24	25
26	27	28	29	30	31	

Are You Really Left-Handed?

Fold your hands together. Which thumb is on top? If you're a lefty, it's probably the right one. For a person who is right-handed, the left thumb will most likely be on top.

AUGUST

Monday

6

Summer Bank Holiday
(Ireland, UK—Scotland, Australia—NSW)
Picnic Day (Australia—NT)

Tuesday

7

Lefty birthday: actor David Duchovny

Wednesday

8

Lefty birthday: actor Keith Carradine

Thursday

9

Lefty birthday: football and baseball player Deion Sanders

Friday

10

Saturday

11

Sunday

12

Lefty birthday: musician Mark Knopfler

August 2012

S	M	T	W	T	F	S
			1	2	3	4
5	6	7	8	9	10	11
12	13	14	15	16	17	18
19	20	21	22	23	24	25
26	27	28	29	30	31	

Born in 1880, Helen Keller became blind and deaf at nineteen months of age from an illness, believed to be scarlet fever or meningitis. Her teacher, Anne Sullivan, brought this brave left-hander back into the human race. Keller was the first deaf and blind person to earn a bachelor of arts degree and became a prolific author and lecturer. Much of her later life was dedicated to raising funds for the American Foundation for the Blind and fighting for people with disabilities. In 1964, she was awarded the Presidential Medal of Freedom, and in 1965 she was elected to the National Women's Hall of Fame.

AUGUST

Monday

13

Lefty birthday: golfer Ben Hogan

Tuesday

14

Wednesday

15

Lefty birthday: French emperor Napoleon Bonaparte

Thursday

16

Lefty birthday: director James Cameron

Friday

17

Lefty birthday: tennis player Guillermo Vilas

Saturday

18

Lefty birthday: actor/director/producer Robert Redford

Sunday

19

Eid al-Fitr

August 2012

S	M	T	W	T	F	S
			1	2	3	4
5	6	7	8	9	10	11
12	13	14	15	16	17	18
19	20	21	22	23	24	25
26	27	28	29	30	31	

Name the Lefties

Q: Which two lefties appeared as employer and
   employee in the film *Up in the Air*?

A: Jason Bateman and Anna Kendrick

AUGUST

Monday

20

Lefty birthday: singer Isaac Hayes

Tuesday

21

Wednesday

22

Lefty birthday: General H. Norman Schwarzkopf

Thursday

23

Lefty birthday: King Louis XVI of France

Friday

24

Lefty birthday: actress Marlee Matlin

Saturday

25

Lefty birthday: singer Billy Ray Cyrus

Sunday

26

Lefty birthday: art collector Peggy Guggenheim

August 2012							September 2012						
S	M	T	W	T	F	S	S	M	T	W	T	F	S
				1	2	3	4						1
5	6	7	8	9	10	11	2	3	4	5	6	7	8
12	13	14	15	16	17	18	9	10	11	12	13	14	15
19	20	21	22	23	24	25	16	17	18	19	20	21	22
26	27	28	29	30	31		23	24	25	26	27	28	29
							30						

The Quotable Lefty

"It is better to stand on the wrong side of the ball and hit it right, than to stand on the right side and hit it wrong."

—motto of the National Association of Left-Handed Golfers

AUGUST-SEPTEMBER

Monday

27

Summer Bank Holiday (UK—except Scotland)

Tuesday

28

Lefty birthday: author Johann Wolfgang von Goethe

Wednesday

29

Lefty birthday: Senator John McCain

Thursday

30

Lefty birthday: baseball player Cliff Lee

Friday

31

Saturday

1

Lefty birthday: boxer Jim Corbett

Sunday

2

Father's Day (Australia, NZ)

September 2012

S	M	T	W	T	F	S
						1
2	3	4	5	6	7	8
9	10	11	12	13	14	15
16	17	18	19	20	21	22
23	24	25	26	27	28	29
30						

Lefty Fun Fact

According to John Odell, curator of history and research at the National Baseball Hall of Fame in Cooperstown, New York, thirteen of the sixty-one enshrined pitchers are left-handed. At 21 percent, that's more than twice the percentage of lefties in the general population.

SEPTEMBER

Monday

3

Labor Day (USA, Canada)

Tuesday

4

Lefty birthday: auto manufacturer Henry Ford II

Wednesday

5

Lefty birthday: cartoonist Cathy Guisewite

Thursday

6

Lefty birthday: explorer Henri de Tonty

Friday

7

Lefty birthday: figure skater Rudy Galindo

Saturday

8

Lefty birthday: comedian Sid Caesar

Sunday

9

September 2012

S	M	T	W	T	F	S
						1
2	3	4	5	6	7	8
9	10	11	12	13	14	15
16	17	18	19	20	21	22
23	24	25	26	27	28	29
30						

Known for his numerous self-portraits, lefty Albrecht Dürer worked as a draftsman in his father's goldsmith workshop before being apprenticed at fifteen to a painter and illustrator. This German painter of the Renaissance was also a wood carver, engraver, and mathematician.

SEPTEMBER

Monday
10

Tuesday
11

Lefty birthday: **actress Kristy McNichol**

Wednesday
12

Lefty birthday: **former Irish prime minister Bertie Ahern**

Thursday
13

Friday
14

Lefty birthday: **actress Joey Heatherton**

Saturday
15

Lefty birthday: **baseball player Nick Altrock**

Sunday
16

Lefty birthday: **actor Ed Begley Jr.**

September 2012

S	M	T	W	T	F	S
						1
2	3	4	5	6	7	8
9	10	11	12	13	14	15
16	17	18	19	20	21	22
23	24	25	26	27	28	29
30						

*Begins at sundown the previous day

Highlights from the History of Left-Handedness

1972: The American Bowling Congress named left-handed bowling champion Patty Costello "Female Bowler of the Year."

SEPTEMBER

Monday

17

Rosh Hashanah*

Tuesday

18

Rosh Hashanah ends

Wednesday

19

Lefty birthday: **songwriter Paul Williams**

Thursday

20

Lefty birthday: **world leader Alexander the Great**

Friday

21

U.N. International Day of Peace

Saturday

22

Lefty birthday: **baseball manager Tommy Lasorda**

Sunday

23

Lefty birthday: **actor Jason Alexander**

September 2012

S	M	T	W	T	F	S
						1
2	3	4	5	6	7	8
9	10	11	12	13	14	15
16	17	18	19	20	21	22
23	24	25	26	27	28	29
30						

*Begins at sundown the previous day

Inspiration from Lefties

Only I can change my life. No one can do it for me.

—Carol Burnett

SEPTEMBER

Monday

24

Lefty birthday: **puppeteer Jim Henson**

Tuesday

25

Lefty birthday: **pianist Glenn Gould**

Wednesday

26

Yom Kippur*

Thursday

27

Friday

28

Lefty birthday: **actor William Windom**

Saturday

29

Lefty birthday: **admiral Lord Nelson**

Sunday

30

Lefty birthday: **Governor Shintaro Ishihara of Tokyo**

October 2012

S	M	T	W	T	F	S
	1	2	3	4	5	6
7	8	9	10	11	12	13
14	15	16	17	18	19	20
21	22	23	24	25	26	27
28	29	30	31			

Lefties Playing Lefties

In the biopic *I'm Not There*, little left-hander Marcus Carl Franklin portrays "Woody Guthrie," an incarnation of fellow southpaw Bob Dylan. This child star was nominated for a 2008 Independent Spirit Award for Best Supporting Male Actor for his performance. Franklin also appeared in *Lackawanna Blues* on HBO, the off-Broadway and Broadway productions of *Caroline or Change*, and the film *Be Kind Rewind*.

OCTOBER

Monday

1

Labour Day (Australia—ACT, NSW, SA)
Queen's Birthday (Australia—WA)

Tuesday

2

Lefty birthday: **spiritual leader Mahatma Gandhi**

Wednesday

3

Thursday

4

Lefty birthday: **baseball player Charlie Leibrandt**

Friday

5

Lefty birthday: **musician and political activist Bob Geldof**

Saturday

6

Sunday

7

Lefty birthday: **Colonel Oliver North**

October 2012

S	M	T	W	T	F	S
	1	2	3	4	5	6
7	8	9	10	11	12	13
14	15	16	17	18	19	20
21	22	23	24	25	26	27
28	29	30	31			

Known as "The Pied Piper of Pounds," "The Clown Prince of Fitness," and "The Apostle of Adipose," Richard Simmons has used his trademark humor and enthusiasm to help millions of people lose weight and embrace a healthy lifestyle. This left-hander grew up in New Orleans with a lefty father and brother and calls himself "a very strict left-hander."

OCTOBER

Monday

8

Columbus Day (USA)
Thanksgiving (Canada)

Tuesday

9

Lefty birthday: linguist Thomas Urquhart

Wednesday

10

Thursday

11

Lefty birthday: football player Steve Young

Friday

12

Lefty birthday: actor Hugh Jackman

Saturday

13

Lefty birthday: singer/songwriter Paul Simon

Sunday

14

October 2012

S	M	T	W	T	F	S
	1	2	3	4	5	6
7	8	9	10	11	12	13
14	15	16	17	18	19	20
21	22	23	24	25	26	27
28	29	30	31			

Inventive Lefties

Thomas Edison

Benjamin Franklin

Elias Howe

Nikola Tesla

OCTOBER

Monday
15

Lefty birthday: tennis player Roscoe Tanner

Tuesday
16

Wednesday
17

Lefty birthday: rapper Eminem

Thursday
18

Lefty birthday: tennis player Martina Navratilova

Friday
19

Lefty birthday: actress Divine

Saturday
20

Lefty birthday: baseball player Keith Hernandez

Sunday
21

Lefty birthday: Israeli prime minister Benjamin Netanyahu

October 2012

S	M	T	W	T	F	S
	1	2	3	4	5	6
7	8	9	10	11	12	13
14	15	16	17	18	19	20
21	22	23	24	25	26	27
28	29	30	31			

The Left Stuff

Started by a left-handed gentleman in 1966, Anything Left-Handed is a shop in the Soho section of London. It has since expanded into a mail-order company and a Left-Handers' Club, with more than 2,000 members. Among the shop's famous customers was Marmaduke Hussey, former chairman of the BBC.

OCTOBER

Monday

22

Labour Day (NZ)

Tuesday

23

Lefty birthday: **soccer player Pelé**

Wednesday

24

United Nations Day

Thursday

25

Lefty birthday: **artist Pablo Picasso**

Friday

26

Eid al-Adha

Saturday

27

Lefty birthday: **journalist Terry Anderson**

Sunday

28

Lefty birthday: **Microsoft founder Bill Gates**

October 2012						
S	M	T	W	T	F	S
	1	2	3	4	5	6
7	8	9	10	11	12	13
14	15	16	17	18	19	20
21	22	23	24	25	26	27
28	29	30	31			

November 2012						
S	M	T	W	T	F	S
				1	2	3
4	5	6	7	8	9	10
11	12	13	14	15	16	17
18	19	20	21	22	23	24
25	26	27	28	29	30	

The Quotable Lefty

"If they sweep with a broom as a left-hander, it's a good bet they'll play better golf as a left-hander."

—Bonnie Bryant

OCTOBER-NOVEMBER

Monday

29

Bank Holiday (Ireland)

Tuesday

30

Wednesday

31

Halloween

Thursday

1

Lefty birthday: baseball player Fernando Valenzuela

Friday

2

Saturday

3

Lefty birthday: actor Jeremy Brett

Sunday

4

Lefty birthday: Captain Jean Danjou

November 2012

S	M	T	W	T	F	S
				1	2	3
4	5	6	7	8	9	10
11	12	13	14	15	16	17
18	19	20	21	22	23	24
25	26	27	28	29	30	

Name the Lefty

Q: One of the earliest recorded left-handers, this world leader is quoted as saying, "I would rather live a short life of glory than a long one of obscurity." Who is he?

A: Alexander the Great

NOVEMBER

Monday

5

Lefty birthday: **pianist Paul Wittgenstein**

Tuesday

6

Election Day (USA)

Wednesday

7

Lefty birthday: **scientist Marie Curie**

Thursday

8

Friday

9

Lefty birthday: **baseball player George Wood**

Saturday

10

Lefty birthday: **King George II of England**

Sunday

11

Veterans' Day (USA)
Remembrance Day (Canada, Ireland, UK)

November 2012

S	M	T	W	T	F	S
				1	2	3
4	5	6	7	8	9	10
11	12	13	14	15	16	17
18	19	20	21	22	23	24
25	26	27	28	29	30	

Did you know that film director Ridley Scott is actually Sir Ridley Scott? Born in South Shields, Tyne and Wear, England, this lefty revolutionized the industry with his striking visual style in the 1982 film *Bladerunner*. Scott has earned Best Director Oscar nominations for *Thelma and Louise*, *Gladiator*, and *Black Hawk Down*. Recently he produced and directed *American Gangster*, *Body of Lies*, and *Robin Hood*.

NOVEMBER

Monday

12

Veterans' Day (observed) (USA)

Tuesday

13

Lefty birthday: comedian and actress Whoopi Goldberg

Wednesday

14

Lefty birthday: actor Brian Keith

Thursday

15

Friday

16

Lefty birthday: Emperor Tiberius

Saturday

17

Lefty birthday: actor Rock Hudson

Sunday

18

Lefty birthday: actor Owen Wilson

November 2012

S	M	T	W	T	F	S
				1	2	3
4	5	6	7	8	9	10
11	12	13	14	15	16	17
18	19	20	21	22	23	24
25	26	27	28	29	30	

Inspiration from Lefties

We make a living by what we get, we make a life by what we give.

—Winston Churchill

NOVEMBER

Monday
19

Lefty birthday: former president James Garfield

Tuesday
20

Lefty birthday: comedian Dick Smothers

Wednesday
21

Lefty birthday: actress Goldie Hawn

Thursday
22

Thanksgiving (USA)

Friday
23

Lefty birthday: comedian Harpo Marx

Saturday
24

Sunday
25

Lefty birthday: lawyer and publisher John F. Kennedy Jr.

November 2012						
S	M	T	W	T	F	S
				1	2	3
4	5	6	7	8	9	10
11	12	13	14	15	16	17
18	19	20	21	22	23	24
25	26	27	28	29	30	

December 2012						
S	M	T	W	T	F	S
						1
2	3	4	5	6	7	8
9	10	11	12	13	14	15
16	17	18	19	20	21	22
23	24	25	26	27	28	29
30	31					

t is widely believed that there are slightly more left-handed boys than girls. Some research has linked left-handedness to the level of testosterone present in the womb before birth, which may explain the imbalance. One thing we do know is that handedness is not a matter of choice, but part of our physiological makeup.

Monday

26

Lefty birthday: baseball player Vernon "Lefty" Gomez

Tuesday

27

Lefty birthday: lawyer and author Caroline Kennedy

Wednesday

28

Lefty birthday: actress Hope Lange

Thursday

29

Lefty birthday: writer/director Joel Coen

Friday

30

St. Andrew's Day (UK)

Saturday

1

Lefty birthday: singer Lou Rawls

Sunday

2

Lefty birthday: tennis player Monica Seles

December 2012

S	M	T	W	T	F	S
						1
2	3	4	5	6	7	8
9	10	11	12	13	14	15
16	17	18	19	20	21	22
23	24	25	26	27	28	29
30	31					

*Begins at sundown the previous day

Lefty Fun Fact

Did you know that one in four Apollo astronauts were left-handed? That's 2.5 times more lefties than in the normal population.

DECEMBER

Monday

3

Lefty birthday: actress Julianne Moore

Tuesday

4

Wednesday

5

Lefty birthday: script supervisor Angela Allen

Thursday

6

Friday

7

Lefty birthday: basketball player Larry Bird

Saturday

8

Lefty birthday: actress Kim Basinger

Sunday

9

Hanukkah*

December 2012

S	M	T	W	T	F	S
						1
2	3	4	5	6	7	8
9	10	11	12	13	14	15
16	17	18	19	20	21	22
23	24	25	26	27	28	29
30	31					

Born Florencia Bisenta de Casillas Martinez Cardona, Vikki Carr's first single, "He's a Rebel," was a hit in Australia, but it took the 1967 release, "It Must Be Him," to shoot Carr to the top of the U.S. charts. Born in El Paso, Texas, she has enjoyed her greatest success singing in Spanish, including winning a 1985 and 1995 Grammy Award for Best Mexican-American Recording and a 1992 Grammy for Latin Pop Album. A benevolent left-hander as well, Carr established the Vikki Carr Scholarship Foundation in 1971. This nonprofit has awarded more than 280 scholarships to students in Texas and California "to help Hispanic students realize their dreams."

DECEMBER

Monday

10

Human Rights Day

Tuesday

11

Lefty birthday: actress Teri Garr

Wednesday

12

Thursday

13

Lefty birthday: actor Dick Van Dyke

Friday

14

Lefty birthday: King George VI of England

Saturday

15

Lefty birthday: baseball player Mo Vaughn

Sunday

16

Hanukkah ends

December 2012

S	M	T	W	T	F	S
						1
2	3	4	5	6	7	8
9	10	11	12	13	14	15
16	17	18	19	20	21	22
23	24	25	26	27	28	29
30	31					

Ninety percent of the human population is right-handed, but in baseball 25 percent of the players, both pitchers and hitters, are left-handed.

—David Peters, Washington University, St. Louis, MO

DECEMBER

Monday

17

Lefty birthday: marathon runner Paula Radcliffe

Tuesday

18

Lefty birthday: actor Brad Pitt

Wednesday

19

Lefty birthday: writer Jean Genet

Thursday

20

Lefty birthday: psychic Uri Geller

Friday

21

Saturday

22

Lefty birthday: baseball player Steve Carlton

Sunday

23

Lefty birthday: actor Brad Hall

December 2012

S	M	T	W	T	F	S
						1
2	3	4	5	6	7	8
9	10	11	12	13	14	15
16	17	18	19	20	21	22
23	24	25	26	27	28	29
30	31					

The Quotable Lefty

"So the next time someone asks how left-handers are different, reply by saying they're special. And that science can prove it."

—David Wolman, *A Left-Hand Turn around the World*

DECEMBER

Monday
24
Christmas Eve

Tuesday
25
Christmas Day

Wednesday
26
Kwanzaa begins (USA)
Boxing Day (Canada, UK, NZ, Australia—except SA)
St. Stephen's Day (Ireland)
Proclamation Day (Australia—SA)

Thursday
27

Friday
28
Lefty birthday: **hockey player Terry Sawchuk**

Saturday
29
Lefty birthday: **cellist Pablo Casals**

Sunday
30
Lefty birthday: **TV personality Matt Lauer**

December 2012						
S	M	T	W	T	F	S
						1
2	3	4	5	6	7	8
9	10	11	12	13	14	15
16	17	18	19	20	21	22
23	24	25	26	27	28	29
30	31					

January 2013						
S	M	T	W	T	F	S
		1	2	3	4	5
6	7	8	9	10	11	12
13	14	15	16	17	18	19
20	21	22	23	24	25	26
27	28	29	30	31		

The Left Stuff

At the Southpaw Shoppe in San Diego, CA, you can buy a wooden ruler with numbers on the left side and in reverse order so you read them from right to left. Printed on the ruler: LEFTIES WILL RULE THE WORLD.

DEC 2012 - JAN 2013

Monday

31

Lefty birthday: **actor Val Kilmer**

Tuesday

1

New Year's Day
Kwanzaa ends (USA)

Wednesday

2

New Year's Day (observed) (NZ)
Bank Holiday (UK—Scotland)

Thursday

3

Friday

4

Saturday

5

Sunday

6

January

February

March

April

May

June

July

August

September

October

November

December

2012

January

S	M	T	W	T	F	S
1	2	3	4	5	6	7
8	9	10	11	12	13	14
15	16	17	18	19	20	21
22	23	24	25	26	27	28
29	30	31				

February

S	M	T	W	T	F	S
			1	2	3	4
5	6	7	8	9	10	11
12	13	14	15	16	17	18
19	20	21	22	23	24	25
26	27	28	29			

March

S	M	T	W	T	F	S
				1	2	3
4	5	6	7	8	9	10
11	12	13	14	15	16	17
18	19	20	21	22	23	24
25	26	27	28	29	30	31

April

S	M	T	W	T	F	S
1	2	3	4	5	6	7
8	9	10	11	12	13	14
15	16	17	18	19	20	21
22	23	24	25	26	27	28
29	30					

May

S	M	T	W	T	F	S
		1	2	3	4	5
6	7	8	9	10	11	12
13	14	15	16	17	18	19
20	21	22	23	24	25	26
27	28	29	30	31		

June

S	M	T	W	T	F	S
					1	2
3	4	5	6	7	8	9
10	11	12	13	14	15	16
17	18	19	20	21	22	23
24	25	26	27	28	29	30

July

S	M	T	W	T	F	S
1	2	3	4	5	6	7
8	9	10	11	12	13	14
15	16	17	18	19	20	21
22	23	24	25	26	27	28
29	30	31				

August

S	M	T	W	T	F	S
			1	2	3	4
5	6	7	8	9	10	11
12	13	14	15	16	17	18
19	20	21	22	23	24	25
26	27	28	29	30	31	

September

S	M	T	W	T	F	S
						1
2	3	4	5	6	7	8
9	10	11	12	13	14	15
16	17	18	19	20	21	22
23	24	25	26	27	28	29
30						

October

S	M	T	W	T	F	S
	1	2	3	4	5	6
7	8	9	10	11	12	13
14	15	16	17	18	19	20
21	22	23	24	25	26	27
28	29	30	31			

November

S	M	T	W	T	F	S
				1	2	3
4	5	6	7	8	9	10
11	12	13	14	15	16	17
18	19	20	21	22	23	24
25	26	27	28	29	30	

December

S	M	T	W	T	F	S
						1
2	3	4	5	6	7	8
9	10	11	12	13	14	15
16	17	18	19	20	21	22
23	24	25	26	27	28	29
30	31					